Jesus Without Christianity

Flynn Barstow

Published by Future Press, 2023.

JESUS WITHOUT CHRISTIANITY

Table of Contents

Introduction

Having taught world religions on the college level for over twenty years, I often found that when we reached the section on Christianity, many students would object to the value of studying the subject. Whenever I questioned them why this was so, the answer would invariably be that they came into the course knowing nothing about Hinduism, Buddhism, Taoism, or Confucianism, so learning about these belief systems was worthwhile. Even Judaism was worth studying because only a small fraction of the class knew about it in any detail. However, they were already familiar with Christianity and considered it judgmental, narrow-minded, and outdated in its thinking. I often found it very challenging to overcome this entrenched viewpoint so that students could see any value in the subject.

For most of the years that I taught this course, I considered this an overreaction on their part, often based on personal and familial experiences that had prevented them from appreciating the belief system. However, over the last eight to ten years, I have come to think that they were right and I was wrong. Over that period, we have all heard many Christians, particularly those of a conservative bent, argue that their values are the only ones that should be adhered to in this country. They have quickly used the levers of politics and government to force these values upon everyone else. These conservative groups have used an idea that has been prevalent from the very beginning in Christianity—that it is the only belief system that knows the truth with a capital T—to push the more liberal and open Christian denominations onto the fringes of religious life.

At the same time as Christianity is hardening into a narrow ideology, more and more people in the Western world are turning away entirely from the Christian view. Numerous studies show that in Western Europe and, more gradually, even the United States, there has been a dramatic decline in those who see Christianity—or any religion, for that matter— playing a significant role in their lives. The great churches of Europe are virtual museums, and recently in the United States, for the first time, agnostics and atheists are equal in number to Roman Catholics. So we see that, as the belief in Christianity steadily declines, many who still believe are fighting a rear guard action by asserting that it is their way or the highway. They are desperately trying to build a dam against a coming tidal wave of change.

I believe they are on the wrong side of history, and their efforts are futile. What will come after the deluge is hard to see, but I suspect Christianity will end up in fifty years or so being predominantly a third-world religion, practiced primarily in Latin America and Africa alongside Islam and other native faiths. What, then, of religious belief in the developed nations of the West? What will remain after the decline of Christianity?

There is no way to delineate the outline of that future accurately. I suspect that it will, in some ways, resemble the pagan systems of belief that existed for thousands of years in Europe and the Middle East before the rise of Christianity. I don't mean that there will be a return to the worship of Zeus and Athena, but I do believe that it will reflect the greater tolerance that existed before the emergence of Christianity. Before Christianity became the Roman Empire's official religion, local areas had their gods, goddesses, and religious practices. Pagan people considered religion to be a result primarily of custom and geography. So those in one location might worship one set of deities, while twenty miles away, another group of gods was worshipped. The people in the first location didn't consider those in the second to be worshipping false gods or to be heretics. The general view was that different groups in different areas would worship other gods unique to their location and society.

You obviously would prefer the ones you had learned about from childhood, but there was an understanding that another form of worship was a matter of geography and culture. You did not consider those who favored a different religion wicked because they saw the world differently from you. Nor did you believe your gods and beliefs were the only correct ones. Paganism was essentially tolerant. You might consider your neighbors odd, or you might be actively curious about their practices. But in any event, you did not think them misguided or evil because their religious views and practices differed from yours.

Rome fought wars for many reasons. For defense, conquest, wealth, and power, but they did not fight wars over religion. When the Romans conquered a people who had a religion different from that of

Rome, they might consider their gods to be stronger. However, they happily incorporated the gods of the defeated into their pantheon. They did not believe them false gods but were weaker than those of Rome.

The only people in the Mediterranean world who thought only their god was a true god were the Israelites. Although a minor people in the Roman world, they compensated for this by believing that only the Hebrew people's god was God. All the others were false and inherently evil. As we shall see, Christianity developed out of Judaism, incorporated this idea with the Hebrew Bible, and became equally intolerant. The Jewish tendency to intolerance was of little significance before the rise of Christianity because Judaism was a religion one was customarily born into, and they did not attempt to convert others to it. Christianity, however, from its very beginnings, was a proselytizing religion, one that sought to gain converts wherever it went. So it spread this intolerance around the Mediterranean and eventually all of Europe. Hence the tolerance of the pagan world disappeared, and religious warfare and hatred were introduced into the West.

The decline of Christianity that is coming will lead to the end of such intolerance, and this will lead to the return of greater openness to a variety of religions and spiritual practices. As I already said, the result is impossible to know in detail. As we see today, I suspect people will follow their spiritual paths, cobbling together belief systems from non-Western religions, literature, philosophy, and science. The results will be eclectic. Some will criticize this approach for lacking discipline and order; others will praise it for not being based on dogma and institutionalized rules. At first, this may be essentially an individual effort engaged in by those on their personal spiritual journeys. Still, given human beings' social nature, small groups will soon form face-to-face or over the internet, and new religions will be developed that are better suited for today.

The point of this writing is to argue that the actual teachings of Jesus should be part of this renaissance of religious practice. Not the Jesus of Christianity, a figure designed by others to become the center of a new mystery cult, but the Jewish preacher who attempted to reform Judaism and make it a universal practice available to all. Once we separate Jesus from Christianity, a movement he neither spawned nor would have approved, we can find considerable wisdom and insight in his teachings for today. I want to show that what Jesus said and did remains a valuable contribution to the future of religion.

Since this book is not intended for scholars but for those engaged in their spiritual and intellectual journey, I have not burdened the text with footnotes. If you have any questions about my assertions, you can quickly check them with a mouse click. My references to the New Testament are all taken from the King James version. My discussion of the life of Jesus is confined to the books of Matthew, Mark, and Luke, with an occasional excursion into the Book of John. The first three books are the synoptic gospels because they give us a bird's eye view of Jesus' life. I have not ventured into discussing the six books of the gospels considered Apocrypha. Early church leaders rejected these because they did not conform to the image of Jesus they wished to promote. However, examining these books may give interested readers a more comprehensive understanding of Jesus' life and teachings.

I have not attempted to be exhaustive in my discussion of Jesus' thoughts. For the purposes of this brief book or long essay, depending on your point of view, I will work with a few of the well-known stories from Jesus' life and hope they will have a renewed value when put in the proper context for even the most skeptical readers.

So, let us begin our spiritual journey by asking, "Where did Christianity Come From?"

Chapter One
The Origins of Christianity

• • • •

YOU MAY THINK THAT the answer to this question is obvious. Didn't Christianity begin with the life and teachings of Jesus? Not really. Jesus himself never explicitly expressed any intention of creating a new religion. If we read the gospels, we get the idea that he was attempting to reform Judaism to make it more open to those who were not born Jews, but he never states that he wished to create a new belief system centered on himself. If you follow the story presented in the New Testament's Book of Acts, the Christian Church only comes into being after Jesus' death when a gathering of the original disciples had a sort of mystical group experience and decided to go forth and preach. Their founding of small religious communities around the Roman world over the next several years led to Christianity. Most believed that Jesus was a human incarnation of the God of the Hebrews.

To understand how this modest, reformist rabbi became an incarnation of God, we have to look critically for a moment at the development of the gospels. First, only the Book of Matthew is named after a disciple who knew Jesus. Although that gospel may be based in part on the reminiscences of that disciple, it was not written down until fifty years after Jesus' death, probably by someone who had learned of Matthew's account, perhaps at second or third-hand. The Book of Mark, probably the first of the gospels to be written, is thought to have been created thirty-five years after Jesus' death, while Luke was composed at the same time as Matthew. Mark is traditionally portrayed as a friend of Peter and not an original disciple, and Luke was a friend of Paul. Neither Luke nor Paul were acquainted with Jesus.

What do we have here, then? We have a series of stories about a traveling teacher that were likely passed on orally within the community of his followers and only written down in the form we have them three to five decades after that leader's death by anonymous authors and editors. This gives them questionable status as historical documents. But the situation is even more complicated because the creators of these gospels considered themselves Christians at a time when there were a variety of competing beliefs as to what constituted Christianity. Each of these writers, therefore, had an ax to grind. Each wanted to argue for his conception of Christianity by creating a Jesus who agreed with his point of view. Hence, although the first three gospels have points of contact, they also diverge widely at times. The Book of Mark, for instance, which was written closest to the death of Jesus, contains no account of a Virgin birth, and scholars tell us the story of the crucifixion and resurrection was only tacked on at the end at a much later date. So two events most central to Christian beliefs do not appear in this earliest account of Jesus' life.

There is another, a towering figure, who must also be considered here to get the complete picture. He is the man who might well be regarded as the actual founder of Christianity: Saul (later Paul) of Tarsus.

Paul was a contemporary of Jesus, but the two never met. Paul was a Pharisee, a group of particularly devout Jews frequently in conflict with Jesus during his lifetime. And Paul was, by his admission, a persecutor of early Christians until he had a conversion experience while on the road to Damascus. After that, he changed his name from Saul to Paul and joined those who claimed to be following Jesus.

Aside from being an indefatigable preacher and letter writer, he also had the advantage of being a citizen of Rome. This was a special distinction, as only about four million of the forty-five million inhabitants of the empire were citizens. This likely means that Paul was much more familiar with Roman culture than the average Jew, and probably why he was chosen by the early community of the followers of Jesus to preach to the Gentiles (those Romans who were not Jewish, which included most of the empire.)

We must pause here to consider the significance of Paul being both a Pharisee and someone well-acquainted with Roman culture. The Pharisees were Jews who believed in a high level of religious devotion. They were extremely proud of their punctiliously following the many complex laws and practices of Judaism. For them, proper religious belief was the most critical aspect of life. We will see in a later chapter that this was almost opposed to the view of Jesus, who valued leading an ethical life over a devout life.

So Paul was an unbending believer in religious practice. Genuine religious faith was the key to getting into heaven. But of equal importance is Paul's knowledge of Roman culture which very likely made him well aware of the Greek and Roman mystery religions that had existed in the Mediterranean world for millennia. The Eleusinian Mysteries, the cult of Dionysus, the Orphic cult, and the cult of Mithras all flourished in the Roman Empire because they promised an afterlife. These religions were prevalent among women and enslaved people, oppressed groups in the Roman world looking for an afterlife to offer them solace for their suffering in their current one. Death and rebirth were at the core of these religions and had at their center a story about the death and resurrection of a god. They also tended to have rituals that included eating the body and drinking the blood of the murdered god.

Suppose it is correct to believe that Paul was aware of these popular Greek and Roman religions. In that case, we can see that when he undertook his mission to preach to the Gentiles, his mind came up with a brilliant fusion of Judaism and the ancient mystery religions, which would appeal to people who were not coming out of the Jewish tradition. Hence he created a new mystery religion in which a new god, Jesus, dies and is reborn. And gradually, the rituals that grew around it were similar to those that the mystery religions had practiced for thousands of years. Paul did not live long enough to see its full development. Still, it is reasonable to argue that he consciously created a religion that took the idea of an afterlife from the mystery religions and put Jesus as the divinity at the center of it. We can only wonder if Paul appreciated the irony of converting pagan

Romans to a faith with a lowly Jew at the center of it as opposed to a Greek god.

For this new religion to become the dominant form of Christianity, it was required that the gospels reflect the divine nature of Jesus. Some evidence for this can be found in the fact that the Gospel of Luke, written by a close friend of Paul, is one that most dramatically develops the divine nature of Jesus. So I contend that those who wrote the gospels were mainly following the thinking of Paul in turning Jesus from a humble rabbi into God.

My point here is that Paul took the person of Jesus and transformed the narrative about him to create a religion that would appeal to Romans looking for a religion that promised an afterlife. This made it very appealing, especially to women and those in the lower classes. An afterlife was not extensively discussed in the ancient Roman religions, and life after death was generally reserved for those with a privileged position in this world that entitled them to be made divine. The idea that immortality was available to all was not customarily accepted. So Christianity, emphasizing everyone having an immortal soul, offered a sort of egalitarian hopefulness that made the religion appealing. In Paul's view, the primary requirement for entering such an eternal life was to believe in Jesus as the incarnation of God and become a Christian. Only by faith in Jesus as being divine, can one tap into this source of immortality.

Although the promise of a road to immortality made Christianity popular, we should not think that it quickly swept through the Roman Empire. It is difficult to get accurate statistics on the number of

Christians in the Roman Empire at any given time, but some scholars think that by 300 C.E., approximately 10% of the Empire was Christian. Whether Christianity would have remained one religion among many or grown to its position of dominance if paganism had been allowed to continue is a matter of speculation. However, in 380 C.E., Emperor Theodosius made Christianity the official religion of the Empire. This meant that only Christianity would receive public funding as a religious institution. Those continuing to practice paganism would lose all chance of advancement in Roman society and be punished. Although it was several hundred years before paganism was stamped out in rural areas, the writing was on the wall. Christianity became more institutional, bureaucratic, and legalistic when it gained the Roman state's support. As I discussed in the Introduction, the intolerance already embedded in Christianity was now supported by the force of law.

Whether Christianity would have been better off if it had never received the support of the Roman state or whether the Western world would have developed more positively if Christianity had remained one religion among others are topics that lead to endless speculation. Another fascinating subject is how paganism might have evolved if allowed to continue once exposed to Christianity. None of this was allowed to happen due to political and historical events.

The central point for us to keep in mind is that Christianity, as conceived of by Paul and as it developed in the three hundred years after the death of Jesus, has almost nothing to do with the teaching of the historical Jesus.

It is to those teachings that we turn in the next chapter.

Chapter Two
The Teachings of Jesus

One of the most challenging issues in discussing the teachings of Jesus is how we can know what he taught. Theologians and philologists have frequently thrown up their hands in despair after attempting to discover what authentically reflects the thoughts of Jesus in the gospels. If, as argued in the last chapter, the gospels were written decades after his death, mainly based on hearsay and by people with a theological ax to grind, what hope is there of discovering the ideas of this wandering rabbi who wrote nothing himself?

I am going to use a common sense rule of thumb. When confronting the life of Jesus, I will always ask, "What is the likelihood that a reform-minded Jew of this period would have said or done something of this sort?" If it looks pretty likely, then I will accept it as a teaching or act of Jesus. When it seems extremely unlikely, I will reject it. When it is borderline, I will remain agnostic about whether it was a part of Jesus' life. I will not attempt to cover every lesson or event described in the synoptic gospels. Instead, as I said in the Introduction, I will limit myself to a few most frequently cited.

I want to start with the claim made by Paul that is central to Christianity, that Jesus was divine. Even with all the best efforts of the authors of the gospels of Matthew and Luke to make Jesus appear godlike by according him a Virgin birth, which is a common trope in many religions before Christianity to make the founder appear divine, they balk at having Jesus overtly declare his divinity. His language remains evasive when pressed on the matter. Because the gospel text is less than conclusive, this had led to extensive theological speculation on why Jesus didn't simply declare his divinity, many seeming to feel that he only refused to do so because he was afraid of incurring the wrath of the Jewish establishment or of the Roman state before he had completed his mission.

I think the answer is far more straightforward. Jesus would never have believed that he was divine. One of the unique attributes of Judaism is that it never considered anyone to be divine except God. For a person to believe himself to be divine was the height of blasphemy in Judaism, then as it is today. Paganism sometimes declared special people, such as the emperor, to be divine, and Greek religion was full of semi-divine individuals. But this was never the approach of Judaism. Abraham and Moses, who in almost any other faith would have been made into gods, remain fully human, even though they are considered prophets and pictured as close to God. For Jews, there is only one God. So it is not credible to believe that a reform-minded Jewish preacher would have thought himself to be an incarnation of God.

Islam, in this regard, has followed Judaism more closely than Christianity. Muslims believe that there is no God but God, and Muhammad is a prophet of God. By making Jesus divine and still claiming to be monotheistic, Christianity has had to perform all sorts of theological contortions. Christians wanted Jesus to be both human and divine. This means you end up believing that Jesus was one in being with God but also fully human, which for nonbelievers seems contradictory. The situation becomes even worse for the Christian when you add the concept of the Holy Spirit, which is also fully divine. Now you have God being three persons: Father, Son, and Holy Ghost. This is the doctrine of the Trinity, which essentially argues that God exists in three persons or aspects but is rooted in one form of being. Jews and Muslims would say this is Christianity's way of having three different divinities without admitting it. Christianity has essentially recognized the impossibility of arguing plausibly for this view by declaring the Trinity to be a mystery and something that must be accepted on faith. Whenever you are told to accept something purely as a matter of faith, you are right to question the foundations of that belief.

Given that Jesus did not believe himself to be divine, what did he think about religion? We can find the core of his belief in his answer to the Pharisees when they asked him what the basic tenets of Judaism were. He answered that believing in God and loving your neighbor as yourself were the essentials of the faith. He doesn't mention visiting the temple regularly or following the elaborate Jewish dietary laws. He says nothing about the hundreds of other ritualistic laws a pious Jew was to follow, which were essential to the Pharisees. He reduces it all to believing in God and being a good person.

Jesus tells us very little about his concept of God. Since he refers to God as his father, we can infer that he experienced a close personal relationship with

God. Jewish belief about God at the time of Jesus took several forms, some holding God to be more aloof from his creation than others. But Jesus seemed to gravitate toward that relationship being a very intimate one. One that required no church structure to mediate between people and God would have been somewhat different from traditional Hebrew temple worship, which relied on the priests to make the appropriate sacrifices to God.

Jesus' emphasis on being a good person, which we mentioned above, is reflected in his story of the Good Samaritan. In summary, the story tells of a Jew who is traveling when he is robbed and badly beaten by bandits. Left for dead by the side of the road, several pious Jews pass by him without bothering to offer any aid. It is a Samaritan who stops to help. He takes the man to an inn, pays for his room, and sees that he is being treated for his injuries. Jesus praised the man's actions, making it clear that religious piety is meaningless unless it eventuates in good actions.

We must also keep in mind a further lesson from this story. The Samaritans had different religious beliefs from traditional Judaism. So what Jesus is also suggesting here is that devotion to a particular religious practice is less important than doing the right thing. It is not your religious faith that will win you merit in the eyes of God, but the goodness of your behavior. Good actions are more important than religious belief, as the Samaritan demonstrates.

Jesus makes this exact point when he refers to the Pharisees as a "whitened sepulcher." A sepulcher is a tomb. So what Jesus is saying is that the Pharisees, with their focus on ritual and outward piety, are like a whitewashed tomb, looking clean and pure on the outside but rotten and corrupt within because they emphasize piety and devotion over doing good works.

Jesus says repeatedly that it is very difficult for a rich man to get into the kingdom of heaven. Part of his reason for saying this is that the rich place more value on gaining pleasure in this life than they do on helping others. Another way this belief manifests itself is in his willingness to associate with non-Jews and those of lower social classes. Rightly or wrongly, Jesus seems to believe that those with little are more willing to share. The Sermon on the Mount in the gospel of Luke also indicates that Jesus considered the poor and downtrodden closer to God.

His willingness to ignore the laws of Judaism, which focused on ritualistic purity arising from dietary rules and associating only with other pious Jews, also made him unpopular with the Pharisees and the Jewish establishment. Jesus felt that what came out of your mouth was more important than what you put into it, and he also thought that good people were to be found in all walks of life. Perhaps, most frequently, among those without wealth or distinction.

It is all very well to say that we should love our neighbors as ourselves, but how do we use this as guidance in our everyday ethical decision-making? A simple set of rules, such as the ten commandments or the over six-hundred laws of Judaism, certainly give more specific guidance than Jesus' somewhat general principle. So how do we operationalize loving our neighbors?

The first point to be clear on here is that Jesus did not believe we should love everyone to the same extent as we love our family and friends. We naturally have a closer emotional attachment to some people than others. What Jesus suggests is that we must take an ethical stance toward everyone who comes into our life. This means that we should always try to act to bring as much benefit as possible into the lives of others. Sometimes this means creating pleasure for others; other times, it means lessening their pain. Jesus is ultimately a proponent of situational ethics. We do not follow a list of prescribed rules but try to determine what is right by following flexible guidelines and adjusting them to meet the facts of the situation. Let me give two examples of this.

There is a famous story in the Gospel of John where a woman who has committed adultery is brought to Jesus. The angry crowd wants to stone her to death because this is the established punishment for such an infraction of Jewish law. Jesus hears the case and suggests that he who is without sin, should cast the first stone. That leads to no one throwing a stone. In fact, everyone slinks away in shame. Jesus then quietly suggests to the woman that she should go forth and sin no more.

How did Jesus' situational ethics work in this case? First, he clarified to the crowd that everyone occasionally does something wrong, which defuses the situation. But then he frees the woman with a relatively mild reprimand. We can guess from his decision that Jesus did not consider adultery a sin worthy of severe punishment. Being exposed as an adulterer in the community was probably punishment enough for the woman. We might ask ourselves hypothetically what Jesus would have done if the woman had been a murderer. Although Jesus might not have condoned her execution, depending on the circumstances of the killing, he may well have felt a harsher punishment was required. In other words, Jewish laws were essential rules of thumb meant to be used as guidelines that could be adapted to different situations.

We see this same approach when the Pharisees come to Jesus and ask whether one should do good deeds on the Sabbath. Remembering that the Jewish Sabbath was meant to be a day where one strictly avoided doing any work, this is a challenging question for Jesus. But he responds without equivocation that the Sabbath is made for man, not man for the Sabbath. He believes that one should always do good works when called for and that doing no work on the Sabbath is merely another rule of thumb or guideline. It can be overridden when more good can be achieved by acting.

In summary, we can see that Jesus did not consider himself divine but rather saw himself as someone breaking down the barriers established by religion. No longer was religious devotion the test of goodness, but instead, the rightness of a person's actions as measured by their tendency to harm or do good to others was to be the essential criterion. Jesus, I think, hoped that his message would be universal, transcending religious divisions and opening the door to greater love between people of different faiths.

Unfortunately, Paul and those who took up the mantle of Christianity turned that message on its head and made belief in the divinity of Jesus the criterion for judging goodness. Making belief in the divinity of Jesus a necessary condition for entering the kingdom of heaven, they widened religious differences and introduced the concept of holy wars, heresy, and religious bigotry into the Western world.

Rarely has the lesson of the founder of religion been so quickly turned on its head and corrupted by his followers, as happened with the teachings of Jesus. If Jesus were to return to earth today, he would doubtlessly say with great sadness that the Pharisees had won. Nor would he look any more kindly on those who attempt to interpret the Bible literally to guide their ethical decisions. Religious devotion and the blind acceptance of formal rules have replaced his message of doing the right thing by acting best for those affected in a given situation. For Jesus, a dose of healthy common sense and caring for others would always be a far better and more compassionate way to go. Let us now consider how Jesus' approach would deal with some of the most pressing issues of our time.

Chapter Three

The Application of the Teachings

Members of the various Christian churches have increasingly gotten involved in politics recently as they attempt to use the law to dictate behavior according to their interpretation of their religion. Usually, they do just what Jesus would not have wanted by creating simple rules governing conduct without genuine concern for the consequences for the people involved. The results are the same whether these rules are based on a Bible reading or some church's historical teachings. People are sacrificed to the worship of rules which are often supported by the flimsiest of historical, theological, and literary evidence. I want to look at a series of issues here and see if our understanding of Jesus, as presented here, will help us arrive at some understanding of what he would like us to do.

Should divorce be allowed?

For a long time, Christianity considered divorce a sin based on a passage in Mark where Jesus argued against the common Jewish teaching that divorce is permitted under the laws of Moses. This seems to be an instance where Jesus goes against his practice of looking at a situation rather than coming up with a blanket rule. However, we need to consider this within its social context. In Judaism at the time, men were far more likely to divorce their wives than the reverse, often for trivial reasons. This often left the woman, who now had no man to give her social standing, at a severe disadvantage in society. I think Jesus feels that banning divorce in most cases, with the possible exception of immorality, protects the downtrodden, in this case, women. He was likely facing a social reality that by allowing divorce, one did not liberate both parties equally to go on to live new lives. The man would be freed to do so, but the woman would lose status and freedom. In today's context, I think Jesus would look at each marriage as a case unto itself and attempt to decide whether ending the marriage would be better overall, taking everyone involved into consideration.

Should abortion be permitted?

Jesus does not speak to this topic, even though abortion was well-known in the ancient world, so that he would have been aware of the practice. The fact that Jesus never declared his views on this topic is probably why Christianity has taken various positions over the millennia. In fact, for much of its history, the Roman Catholic Church followed Aristotle in the view that only when the fetus has a soul, which happens forty days after conception for male fetuses and ninety days after for females, did it become a human being. The Book of Genesis presents the even more stringent requirement that only after birth and the taking the first breath of air is the fetus a human being. My point here is that the view that the fetus is a human from conception has only recently become the accepted view among some Christians.

Given what we have learned about Jesus' approach to moral issues, I think he would judge each instance on a case-by-case basis by examining the consequences for all involved in carrying the fetus to term. I can easily imagine him thinking that, in some instances, an abortion would be morally wrong, while in others, it would be justified.

However, the most crucial point here is to reflect on Jesus' suspicion of religious institutions and their tendency to legislate morality for the individual. He would oppose any religious or political body stepping in to determine the rightness or wrongness of actions of moral consequence. He is a firm believer that institutions tend to corrupt by laying down unswerving laws that ignore significant moral differences in situations. The major decisions in a person's life should be left up to them because, ultimately, they are the ones who will be held accountable.

What was Jesus's view of government?

This is another topic that Jesus did not discuss at length. The most famous instance he mentions is in the Gospel of Mark, where the Pharisees ask Jesus whether they must pay taxes. Jesus replies that they should "Render unto Caesar what is Caesar's and unto God what is God's. In line with Jesus' general suspicion of institutions, I think he was saying that church and state should remain separate. That would mean churches should not become involved in politics, and governments should not interfere in religion. We find that both of these barriers are increasingly being breached today as churches attempt to use the law to enforce their ethical beliefs, and governments often use the law to support the churches of their choice. I think Jesus thought that religious faith was personal and that using force to convert people would diminish their steadfast commitment to their beliefs and force others to espouse false views.

When using the levers of power to enforce your beliefs, one should always consider whether you are willing to set a precedent where the same will be done to you when those with differing views come into power.

A corollary of this division between government and religion is that Jesus also thought there should be a high wall between the sacred and the secular. We see this most clearly when Jesus drives the moneylenders out of the temple. He was aware of the dangers of religious institutions becoming commercial enterprises. Today with the growth of corruption in megachurches and the scandal at the Vatican Bank, we should listen to his message. When a church becomes commercialized, it quickly becomes an institution that exists more for the benefit of those who staff its bureaucracy than its members.

Indeed, Jesus is generally suspicious of organized religion because he was aware that Judaism as an institution had slowly become more of a political and commercial organization than a religious one. That may well be why he expressed his relationship with God as a personal one that thrived outside of any organizational setting.

What was Jesus' view of the afterlife?

Here we are confronted with a dilemma because, as we mentioned earlier, the followers of Paul wanted to create a new mystery religion. At the core of any such faith was the belief in personal immortality. So we can't know how much of the discussion of an afterlife in the gospels can be accurately attributed to Jesus and how much was added by the followers of Paul. A further problem is that Jews at the time of Jesus had different views on whether there was an afterlife, so as a Jew, Jesus may or may not have been committed to this belief.

All I think that we can safely say here is that unlike the Christian Church that followed, Jesus himself never believed that faith in him as an incarnation of God was required to achieve eternal life. If Jesus did believe in an afterlife, he would likely have thought that it was earned by living a good life and not as a consequence of believing in the "right" religion.

What was Jesus' view of God?

As I already indicated in the last chapter, it is likely that Jesus, as a devout Jew, believed in the God of the Hebrew Bible or the Christian Old Testament. But as I noted, he seems to have had a particularly close and personal relationship with God, demonstrated by his tendency to call him father. Beyond this, however, Jesus gives us very little information about his precise conception of God. This raises a question. If we reject the Hebrew/Christian image of God, must we necessarily reject the teachings of Jesus? I think not. Very little of what Jesus teaches in his parables is linked to a definite image of God. Aside from the view that God is an ethical being who cares about people, there is no restriction on how a follower of Jesus may think about God.

But what if you are agnostic on the question of God's existence? Or what if you think that there is an ultimate intelligence in the universe but believe humans can have no reliable idea of what such a being is like or wants? Does this mean you must reject the lessons of Jesus? I don't think this is the case. Most of what Jesus teaches concerns how we should treat others. Even if you are unsure whether there is a God or an afterlife, you can still learn a lot about how to be a good person from what Jesus has to say.

You may think that if there is no afterlife offering a reward for being good, why should you bother? The answer to this question is that each of us has only one life to live, and how we lead that life will be remembered. That is our certain immortality in this world. Therefore, we may still want to leave behind within the memories of others who live on after us an image of ourselves as people of goodwill and integrity. A bad person may be able to evade the law, but the headline of their obituary will be punishment enough.

Did Jesus' crucifixion and resurrection take place?

As I mentioned earlier, the Book of Mark, the gospel written closest to the time of Jesus' life, has been shown to have a crucifixion and resurrection story that was only added at a much later date. This suggests that, for some reason, the original writer of Mark did not include it to begin with. It is hard to know why he would leave out such a crucial moment unless it never took place. New Testament Apocrypha also suggests that Jesus did not die on the cross.

My inclination—although not a certainty—is to believe that Jesus was crucified. He raised issues that were discomforting to the authorities, and crucifixion was a common form of execution among the Romans and other ancient peoples. More convincingly, there is also clearly a belief on the part of Jesus' earliest followers that he was crucified, so he may indeed have run afoul of the authorities and been executed, whether in the dramatic way depicted in some of the gospels or not, it is difficult to know.

The more critical issue is whether he was resurrected. Here we enter again into the land of the followers of Paul. As mentioned several times, they needed a narrative in which the god arose from the dead. This would guarantee the appeal of Christianity to the Gentiles and remind them of their traditional mystery religions. They wanted the fact of the resurrection to be beyond doubt, so they had Jesus appear after death in bodily form to many people before ascending into heaven.

One can believe this, depending on your willingness to accept miraculous events only attested to by those committed to promoting the new religion. My view of Jesus as only human does not require that we give up the possibility of personal immortality. It simply means that we cannot turn to the story of Jesus' life as evidence for its existence. There may still be good philosophical, scientific, and religious arguments for believing in life after death, but these must be considered separately from the Christian narrative.

What was Jesus' view of miracles?

Although the gospels are always careful to say that this power came from God and not from Jesus himself, if the gospels are to be believed, he performed many of them. Many more are attributed to his followers after the crucifixion. These fall into roughly three categories: psychological miracles, physical miracles, and natural world miracles.

By psychological miracles, I mean those referred to in the gospels as the driving out of evil spirits. There are many cases in which people obviously suffering from severe mental distress come to Jesus, who cured them of their affliction. It is difficult to know how many such events were added by later followers of Paul to reinforce Jesus's divine status. But some of these accounts might be true because people, even today, sometimes experience at least temporary relief from their mental illness when confronted by a charismatic individual in an emotionally heated environment.

By physical miracles, I mean cases where people are cured of a physical illness by coming into contact with Jesus. As mentioned above, it is difficult to know how many of these stories were added later to buttress the claims of the early founders of the religion. These are a bit more difficult to accept than psychological miracles, but again, we are aware today of the influence the mind has on the body, so it is possible that Jesus was able to cure some physical illnesses, at least temporarily, in this way,

The raising of Lazarus from the dead is a unique and particularly troubling event. First, it seems to be a less easily explained event than most others, assuming that Lazarus was truly dead and not simply catatonic in some way. Secondly, there is the ethical issue of bringing someone back from the dead simply because they are a friend. This sort of preferential treatment is disturbing. Everyone mourns the death of a loved one; why should someone who happens to be especially close to Jesus be brought back while all the others who passed away at the same time remain dead? I suspect whoever wrote the Gospel of John never considered this because their focus was on asserting that Jesus had all the powers of God, including the ultimate one of granting life.

The final class of miracles is the natural. The best example of this is in the Gospel of John. While attending a wedding that runs out of wine, Mary, the mother of Jesus, implores him to perform a miracle. He reluctantly does so by turning water into wine. This is also a disturbing miracle for two reasons. First is its rather frivolous nature. No one is cured, healed, or saved from death. This miracle simply allows the party to continue. Secondly, it is genuinely an event counter to science, where we cannot attribute its success to Jesus' influence on the human mind.

I don't think we should let the presence of miracles in the story of Jesus' life prejudice us against taking his teachings seriously. The followers of Paul doubtlessly added many to support their claim for the divinity of Jesus, and others can be explained in scientific ways. But should we doubt the possibility of miracles in the first place? Unexplained events often do happen even today. Sometimes seemingly unexplainable good things do happen. Of course, sometimes equally baffling bad things happen, although we do not usually think of these as miracles. I do not think a belief system based on miracles is sustainable, but we should be open to the possibility that things we don't currently understand can occur.

In the long run, they are not essential to appreciating Jesus' teachings. The topic of the last chapter is how we can develop this appreciation further.

Chapter Four
A Glance at the Future

As I mentioned in the introduction, I have not attempted to give an exhaustive examination of Jesus' teachings. Many more parables make essential points about his thoughts and beliefs. I have tried in this concise book to clear away some of the theological ground so that a person making their spiritual journey can come to appreciate the teachings of Jesus without the heavy emotional baggage that comes when one associates him with Christianity.

To sum up, briefly, Jesus tried to break down the religious barriers between Jews and non-Jews by focusing on universal ethical principles that can be applied situationally to help arrive at results that are best for those affected. The moral life is balancing gains and losses in a given situation to bring about the most good or least harm for those involved. This is what Jesus means by loving our neighbors as ourselves. We do not allow prejudice, selfishness, and social class limitation to prevent us from considering each life essential and deserving consideration. This common-sense view is what Jesus espoused and tried to teach using his parables.

As I mentioned in the introduction, Christianity is a set of religious institutions slowly fading away in the Western world. Still, the message of Jesus, if properly separated from these institutions, continues to have a great potential to guide people throughout life. It remains challenging to follow in his footsteps because he does not make things easy. He calls us to rise above our baser nature and take a more distanced view of our place in the world. He asks that we become less wrapped up in ourselves and more a part of a large social, natural, and cultural environment.

What next step do I recommend for someone who has read this book and found it interesting? I suggest reading Matthew, Mark, Luke, and John and then giving some thought to the parables, particularly those that relate to how we should interact with others. Although Jesus was not a big fan of institutions, he would approve of people getting together online or informally in person and discovering his message, much as he did with the disciples. Many people would find it helpful to discuss the application of his teachings to the problems in their own lives, particularly with the gentle guidance of others who are also trying to understand his teachings.

This conversation could also expand beyond the teachings of Jesus to those of other religious thinkers, philosophers, and even fiction writers. We are at the beginning of a great adventure that will require us to discover new ways of understanding our place in the universe, but it would be foolish not to build on the lessons of the past. And this certainly includes the teachings of Jesus.

Printed in Dunstable, United Kingdom